Everything You Need to Know About

Virginity

If you are unsure about losing your virginity, it is probably better to wait.

Everything You Need to Know About

Virginity

Michael A. Sommers
Annie Leah Sommers

The Rosen Publishing Group, Inc.
New York

To Our Jeb

Published in 2000 by The Rosen Publishing Group, Inc.
29 East 21st Street, New York, NY 10010

Copyright © 2000 by The Rosen Publishing Group, Inc.

First Edition

Library of Congress Cataloging-in-Publication Data

Sommers, Michael A., 1966–
    Everything you need to know about virginity / by Michael A. Sommers and Annie Leah Sommers.
        p. cm. -- (The need to know library)
    Includes bibliographical references and index.
    Summary: Discusses the issues surrounding virginity for teens, dispels myths about it, and helps teens decide for themselves how to express their sexuality.
    ISBN 0-8239-3115-3
    1. Sexual ethics for teenagers—Juvenile literature. 2. Virginity—Juvenile literature. 3. Sexual abstinence—Juvenile literature. 4. Teenagers—Sexual behavior—Juvenile literature. [1. Sexual ethics. 2. Sexual abstinence. 3. Youth—Sexual behavior.] I. Sommers, Annie Leah, 1968– II. Title. III. Series.
HQ35 .S56 2000
306.7'0835--dc21

                                                                99-056218

Manufactured in the United States of America

Contents

Introduction

*J*ocelyn looked at her watch and saw that it was almost midnight. She hoped that her parents were already sound asleep because Jimmy would be arriving soon. Waiting made her antsy. Jocelyn decided to put on some more perfume. She sprayed her armpits and reached down and dabbed it on the top of her thighs.

Earlier that evening, after taking a long bath, Jocelyn had practiced inserting the diaphragm inside her vagina. Although she had been practicing for days, she still wasn't sure if she was doing it the right way. Even though she knew that a diaphragm was considered a safe form of birth control, Jocelyn still worried about getting pregnant. She hoped that Jimmy wouldn't forget to *bring condoms. At first, he had refused to wear one. "What's the danger if we're both virgins?" he had said to her. But Jocelyn had stood her ground. "No condoms, no sex," she had warned him, knowing that Jimmy wanted to "do it" so badly that he would agree to almost anything.*

Jocelyn paced up and down her room and thought of what was going to happen next. The fact that her parents were downstairs made her really uncomfortable. They'd have to be extra quiet. If her parents found out, they'd kill her.

She actually had no idea what it would be like to have sex with Jimmy. It dawned on her that she'd never even touched his penis. And, come to think of it, she wasn't even sure she wanted to. It seemed kind of gross.

Jocelyn loved Jimmy. Or, at least, she thought she did. She'd never told him she loved him. Nor had he told her. But Jimmy had said that sex is a natural expression of love. So that must mean he loved her if he wanted to lose his virginity with her. She had thought she wanted to lose her virginity, too. But if so, why was she so nervous?

Whether you lose it or choose it, virginity is a big deal for any teenager. In fact, the decision of whether or not to remain a virgin is probably more complicated today than ever before. Sexually transmitted diseases (STDs) such as chlamydia, gonorrhea, and herpes have always existed. So has the risk of accidental teen pregnancy. But the tendency for teens to start having sex at a younger age, and more often, increased these risks. Then, in the 1980s, the emergence of AIDS made sex suddenly scary.

While religious organizations, parents, and politicians began making noise about the dangers of premarital sex, the media, the entertainment industry, and all kinds of commercials and advertisements showed nonstop images of gorgeous couples in various stages of "getting it on." These days the pressure to be—or not to be—a virgin is enormous.

The notion of virginity—of someone who has not had sexual intercourse—has been around throughout history. It is a notion that exists in all cultures and all religions and one that has generated many beliefs and myths. Some of these beliefs are legitimate, whereas others—such as myths—are false. Whether or not you remain a virgin, it is important to make an educated decision based on the facts and your own feelings.

If you decide to remain a virgin, that's great. It means you are mature enough to recognize that you're not ready yet. Especially for guys, one's virginity used to be an issue shamefully left in the closet, but recently, a handful of groups supporting teenage abstinence have made "coming out" as a virgin much easier.

If you decide the time is right to lose your virginity, that's great, too. It means you feel secure about your

Virgins are often dressed in white in literature and films, such as Meg Ryan's character in *Joe Versus the Volcano*.

sexual self and want to express it physically with another person to whom you are emotionally and sexually attracted. Sex isn't bad—it's extremely natural. If it occurs safely and smartly, under the right circumstances and with the right person for the right reasons, it can be a wonderful experience.

Sexuality is one of the most fundamental aspects of being human. This is why, basically, everybody under the sun has an opinion to give. It's healthy to be exposed to these points of view—the more the better—because the worst thing one can do is keep from talking about sex or sexuality at all. Whether you decide to be a virgin or not, keep the lines of communication open, be honest, and be informed. This book is organized with that goal in mind. It doesn't pretend to give answers—the answers are for you to discover. But it does aim to expose you to as much information and as many different points of view as possible.

Chapter One

What Is a Virgin?

The word "virgin" first appeared in the thirteenth century, most frequently in reference to a young woman who has never had sexual intercourse. The word virgin also has other meanings: A virgin rainforest is one that is untouched by humans; extra virgin olive oil is extracted in such a way that it is extremely pure. Likewise, society tends to see virgin girls as pure, innocent, and unspoiled.

This does not mean that only heterosexual young women are virgins. Anyone who has never had sex—whether a guy or a girl, gay or straight—can be considered a virgin. Virginity is associated mostly with heterosexual girls for two reasons. First, virginity traditionally has been, and still is, viewed from society's

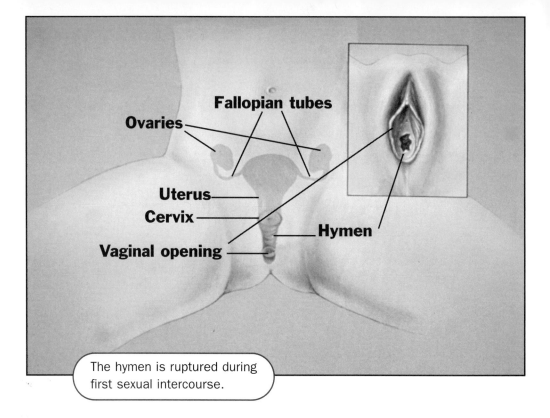

The hymen is ruptured during first sexual intercourse.

dominant male and heterosexual perspective. A girl is considered to have lost her virginity only when a male penis has penetrated her. And the second reason: On penetration, a girl's hymen is ruptured. This usually causes bleeding, which has long been considered proof of intercourse.

For guys, there is no such proof. Physically, the penis remains exactly the same before and after the deed. And a male probably won't experience any of the physical discomfort that a female partner may feel. This lack of tangible proof also generally applies to gays and lesbians who have sex for the first time.

No matter what your sex or sexuality, losing your virginity represents an enormous change in your life.

Symbolically, it is a rite of passage, from childhood to adulthood. Emotionally, it means discovering and dealing with a whole new range of complicated feelings and becoming familiar with your body and your desires (as well as those of your partner). Practically, it means taking responsibility for your own health and the health of your partner.

Losing your virginity is not a decision to be taken lightly. If you do decide to have sex, think about it, talk about it, educate yourself about it, and make sure you're completely comfortable with the idea. Make sure you're doing it for yourself—not because you're being pressured by your partner or your friends.

Orlando's buds were always bragging about the girls they had scored with. His friend Roger had a list of girls he had "done." Rog was trying to make it to fifty by the time the school year ended.

Orlando always got quiet when the guys talked about sex. He had gone out with a few girls, but he had never gone all the way.

One day after school, Rog came up to Orlando, who was hanging outside the school with Max and Joaquim.

"Orlando, man," said Rog, putting his arm around Orlando's shoulder.

"What's up, dude? Goin' through a dry spell, huh?"

"What do you mean, Rog?" asked Orlando.

"Seems to me like it's been a while since you've gotten some. Am I right or am I right?"

"You're right, Rog," said Max. "The guy's been in the middle of the Sahara for months now."

All the guys started cracking up. Orlando felt embarrassed.

"Hey, Orlando, don't worry, man. Tonight I'll take you with me to Peg's party, and I'll make sure you score."

That night at Peg's party, Rog introduced Orlando to Elena. "She's amazing, dude. Plus, she thinks you're cute," Rog whispered in Orlando's ear.

Orlando thought Elena was nice enough and pretty good-looking. They talked about school and about how cool Rog was. Then Elena led Orlando into Peg's mom's bedroom and asked him if he wanted to have sex. Orlando nervously said yes.

Five minutes later, it was all over. Elena looked disappointed and Orlando felt like an idiot for having ejaculated so soon. It hit him that he had just lost his virginity—with a girl he didn't even know. He realized he had done so more to impress Rog than because he had wanted to. The thought really depressed him.

When you are in your teens, the issue of virginity probably will become a big deal. This is partly because of the effects of your changing body and newly awakened

Friends often pressure one another to have sex before they're ready.

hormones. You will experience both sexual desire and attraction to others. Such discoveries can be very exciting. They also can be confusing. So many changes and so much newness can make you vulnerable. This is why it's important to educate yourself as much as possible about sex and all of the complicated feelings and consequences that accompany it. This will help you to make wise decisions about whether you feel ready to have sex.

Losing your virginity is a big deal. But it doesn't mean that you're automatically transformed from a pure and innocent creature into a pervert. Neither does it mean that you automatically go from being a nerd to being cool.

The History of Virginity

The term "virgin" was first used in ancient Greece and Rome in reference to a woman—or a goddess—who was independent, in the sense that she wasn't the property of any man. It was only later that virginity meant sexual virginity. The most famous virgin is the Virgin Mary, mother of Jesus Christ. She is a central figure in Christianity, and her virginity is of key importance. With the spread of Christianity throughout the Western Hemisphere, both Mary and virginity came to be thought of as sacred. The impact of 2,000 years of Christianity has left its mark on contemporary Western culture. For this reason, even today, in most European countries as well as in North and South America (places where

The Virgin Mary is a central figure of Christian religions.

Christianity is the dominant religion), society still tends to place great symbolic importance on a girl's virginity.

With the Virgin Mary as a role model for most Western women, it is little wonder that virginity became an important trait for a young, unmarried woman. Being a virgin before marriage meant you were pure and unspoiled for your husband. Not being one meant you were damaged goods. Because, traditionally, a woman's role has been to marry and raise children, only when she was married was a young bride allowed and expected to lose her virginity.

During the Middle Ages, when Christianity was spreading throughout Europe, there were many theories and myths about ways of testing for virginity. It was believed that you could detect a virgin by the color of her urine (a virgin's was clear and sparkling) or by the direction in which her breasts pointed (a virgin's breasts pointed up, toward Heaven). In medieval romances, magical objects were used to test for virginity. A common test relied on a magic drinking horn. A horn was filled with blood-colored wine, and if the woman drinking from it was not a virgin, the wine would spill.

The Hymen
During the same period, gynecological reports declared an unbroken hymen to be a sign of virginity. The hymen is the thin piece of tissue that partly blocks the entrance to the vagina. It is popularly known as "the

cherry." Some girls are born without a hymen, but most have one, although it can vary in shape and size. The word comes from the name of the Greek god of marriage. It was thought—and still is—that because the hymen blocked the vaginal opening, it would remain unbroken unless a girl had sexual intercourse.

In many cultures, it is a serious crime for an unmarried woman to be found with a ruptured (broken) hymen. Among some Australian tribes, an older woman punctures a young bride's hymen one week before her marriage. If the hymen is already separated from the vaginal walls, the woman is humiliated, tortured, and even killed. This is tragic, especially when you consider that the hymen can be separated for reasons that have nothing to do with sexual intercourse. Inserting a tampon, masturbating, strenuously stretching your body—all of these activities can rupture the hymen. On the other hand, it may be very hard for the hymen to rupture. Some women must have their hymens removed by surgery before the birth of their first child because the hymen didn't break during intercourse.

When the hymen is separated—whether during first intercourse or at some other time—there may be some slight bleeding and a little pain. Both are quite normal and both usually stop after a short time. Some women experience no discomfort at all during this process.

Chapter Two | The Ins and Outs of Sexuality

Before you hit puberty, life was probably a lot simpler. As you go through your teenage years, you will begin to discover your own body and sexuality, as well as those of others. This awareness, and the feelings that accompany it, is what sexuality is all about. Although both guys and girls change, develop, and become aware of their sexuality at roughly the same time, the changes that each goes through are sometimes quite different.

Male Puberty

With guys, puberty can begin anywhere from age eleven to fifteen. From this point on, your body starts to grow and develop. You'll get taller and more muscular, and your face, chest, arms, legs, and underarms will begin to sprout hair. So will the area around your

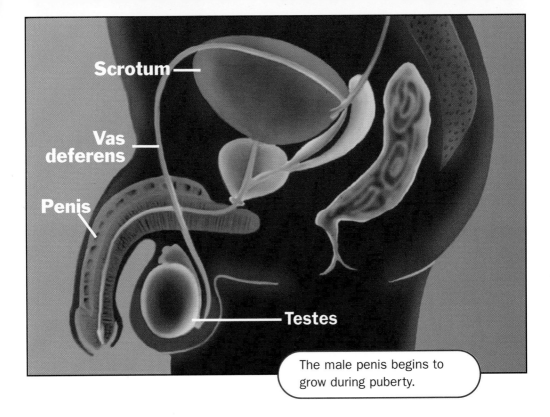

Scrotum

Vas deferens

Penis

Testes

The male penis begins to grow during puberty.

penis—this is called pubic hair. Around this time, your penis will start to grow. Many people make a big deal about penis size. The fact is, size isn't a big deal. On average, a full-grown penis is usually between 3 1/4 and 4 1/4 inches long when flaccid (limp) and 5 to 7 inches long when erect.

When puberty hits, you'll find yourself getting erections. An erection happens when your penis fills with blood and gets hard. Erections usually occur when you get sexually aroused, but you also might get them for no reason at all. These are called spontaneous erections and are very common, so there's no reason to get embarrassed about them. Erections might last anywhere from a few seconds to a few minutes, or longer.

At night, you might get an erection and even ejaculate in your sleep. You might wake up thinking that you have wet your bed. In reality, what you've had is a nocturnal emission, or a wet dream. And the sticky fluid that came out of your penis isn't urine, but semen. Semen contains sperm and urine doesn't. The way that your body works, you can't urinate and ejaculate at the same time.

While your penis develops, so will the sac that hangs under it, the scrotum. Your scrotum houses both of your testicles. Testicles produce sperm and also the male hormone called testosterone. As you advance through puberty, your testicles will get bigger and hang lower. Don't worry if one hangs lower than the other—this is normal. Do worry about protecting your testicles from getting hit. As anyone who has ever been "kicked in the balls" can attest, the testicles are very sensitive.

Female Puberty

Girls often reach puberty before boys do—experiencing the first outward changes anywhere between the ages of eight and fourteen—and for girls, puberty can last longer, too. Not only will you grow taller, but your hips, thighs, and bottom will begin to fill out. As your breasts develop (a little or a lot—all sizes are possible and normal), your nipples will get larger. Around the same time, your first pubic hair will begin to grow, followed by

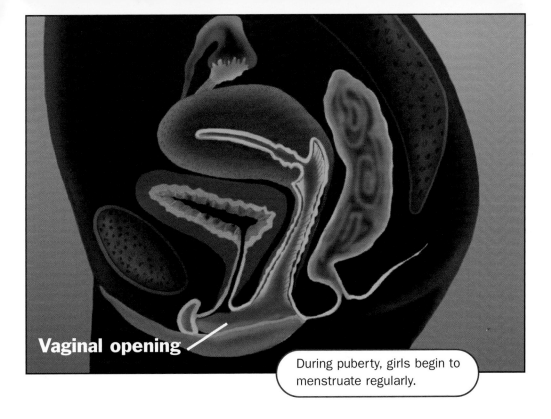

Vaginal opening

During puberty, girls begin to menstruate regularly.

underarm hair. And soon after, your hormones will cause your vagina to produce a whitish discharge, which is simply part of a natural cleansing process.

Between the ages of ten and sixteen, most girls will probably experience their first menstrual period. Your period is neither an illness, nor anything of which to be ashamed. Many societies view a girl's first period as a rite of womanhood and, biologically, a period is an essential part of your reproductive cycle.

Once a month, an egg matures in your ovaries and travels down a fallopian tube to your uterus, or womb. Your uterus is a hollow, pear-shaped organ that is so flexible it can expand to contain a full-grown fetus. In preparation for the egg's monthly arrival, the lining of the uterus becomes thick and soft in anticipation of the egg being fertilized by a sperm and developing into a fetus. If no sperm are in sight, the uterus flushes out this spongy lining, along with some blood, body fluids, and the disintegrated egg.

This reddish menstrual fluid flows out of your body from between three to six days each month, although it might take a couple of years before your period arrives with regularity. Once you've become sexually active, missing a period can be a sign of pregnancy. However, it also can be due to stress, a change in diet, an increase in exercise, a large change in your normal routine, travel, or use of certain drugs.

Your period may sometimes be accompanied by mild to severe cramps, headaches, pimples, nausea, and food cravings. It also can be preceded by feelings of anxiety or depression that are due to hormonal changes. These feelings are common and are part of PMS (premenstrual syndrome).

Male and Female Sexuality

Hormones such as testosterone (mostly found in guys) and estrogen (mostly found in girls) are not only responsible for the changes in your bodies and sexual organs, but for the changes in your emotions and desires—many of which are linked to both sex and your sense of sexuality.

Exploring your sexuality is all about exploring yourself as a sexual being. Your developing sexual organs will give you a sense of maleness or femaleness that is strange at first but that will also be the source of pride and pleasure. Becoming intimate with your changing body and the way it works is important. It's essential to feel comfortable with your body and to know your body well enough to be able to detect any changes that occur that might or might not become health problems.

Both males and females have parts of their bodies that are particularly sensitive. When touched, these parts can become aroused. Such regions are known as erogenous zones. Although different people have different erogenous zones—some people may get excited by having their toes fondled, others by having the backs of their knees caressed—male and female sexual organs tend to be particularly sensitive. For males, touching, fondling, or rubbing your penis and testicles can be very arousing. For females, your clitoris—the round bulge located high up between the soft protective folds of skin known as the labia minor (inner lips)—is a sexual hot spot, full of nerve endings that are easily aroused. Other intimate and sensitive regions include nipples, breasts, and the anus.

When, and whether, you decide to let a partner touch these intimate regions is up to you. Meanwhile, exploring these erogenous zones on your own can be an important part of discovering your likes and dislikes. Touching your genitals for sexual pleasure is known as masturbation. Although it is seen as wrong in some societies and religions, masturbation is seen by many other people as neither dirty nor perverted. The experience brings physical pleasure, and in the event that your masturbation climaxes in an orgasm, it will give you a sense of sexual release. Masturbating also can help make you a more knowledgeable lover when you do decide to engage in sexual activity.

As you become aware of your own sexuality, you will also become aware of the sexuality of guys and girls around you. You might find that you are attracted to a member of the opposite sex. In this case, you are probably heterosexual. However, you may be attracted to someone of the same sex. If this is the case, you may be homosexual. You might even be aroused by people of both sexes. This is called bisexuality.

Leila was confused. She loved her boyfriend, Bruce. Or, at least, she thought she did. They got along really well. But often, when they fooled around, Leila found herself feeling distant. It was as if she was going through the motions, but the feelings were missing. There was a complication—Katherine. Katherine was Leila's lab partner in chemistry. They had so much fun—blowing up beakers, steaming up the classroom with yellow vapor, and laughing a lot. Leila felt a special bond with Katherine, and she hated the days when they didn't have chemistry.

Earlier that week, the girls had gone to Katherine's house to study for a midterm exam. They had ended up sitting on Katherine's bed and staying up all night talking about everything under the sun. At one point, Katherine had started caressing Leila's face, and then her chest. Leila was shocked, but at the same time very aroused. She wondered if she liked Katherine better than she did Bruce. And if so, was it just a case of liking one person better than another? Or could it be that she was a lesbian?

In your teenage years especially, it is common to have feelings for and even experiment sexually with members of both sexes. Remember, this is a time of great change, when you are trying to define what you like and don't like. Although most people define themselves as heterosexuals, this does not mean that homosexuals or bisexuals are sick or abnormal. Homosexuality is simply another way of loving. Although it does not constitute what society sees as the norm—i.e., the most common form of sexual behavior—it is nothing about which to feel guilty. Homosexuals are no less men or women, masculine or feminine, than are heterosexuals.

If you're not sure if you're straight, gay, or "bi," don't worry. What matters is staying open to your true feelings. You don't even have to decide into what category you fit. You can make up your own name for your sexuality. After all, it is your own and it's something for you to enjoy, not to agonize over.

Chapter Three | Teenage Virgins Speak Out

In the period that followed the sexually liberated '60s and '70s, many North American adults—ranging from teachers and preachers to parents and politicians—expressed anxiety over the fact that teens were having their first sexual experiences at an increasingly young age. In many schools, condom dispensers were installed in bathrooms. It was hoped that such easy access to protection would ensure that the large number of teens who admitted to having sex were having safe sex. Unfortunately, an alarming number were not. Unplanned pregnancies and STDs were increasing, and a lethal sexually transmitted virus called HIV was causing thousands of deaths.

Now, at the start of the new millennium, there appears to have been a change in the sexual behavior

Virginity can seem preferable to teenage pregnancy.

of many teens. In the United States, magazine covers promise to give the scoop on teen virgins. And, believe it or not, many of these articles focus on male virgins. This is a far cry from the time when guys were rumored to spend much of their spare time discussing how often they had scored.

It is not unusual to know or hear about young women who remain virgins until they are married. Usually these women are respected, not ridiculed. Even famous Hollywood actresses have admitted to being virgins. But guy virgins? There was a time when men who ate quiche were considered to be less than masculine. And now, all of a sudden, it's cool for guys to be virgins, too. What is going on?

Why So Many Teen Virgins?

According to the Princeton Religion Research Center, virginity is making a comeback in high schools and on college campuses. A recent study carried out by the center found that 46 percent of Americans believe that premarital sex is wrong. Two years earlier, the results of the same survey had been 39 percent. A key factor in this trend is the growing concern over the risk of contracting an STD or AIDS, or becoming pregnant. However, most teens explain their decision to remain virgins by citing religious, moral, or just plain personal reasons.

Although Malcolm, eighteen, never planned on being a virgin, at a certain point he realized that sex before marriage wasn't something his parents supported. "That's probably part of the reason I decided to be a virgin," he admits. "But more than that, I just can't understand going out and 'knockin' boots' with someone you just met.

"I've been with Sherry for over six months and sometimes we both get tempted to do it. But I've thought about it a lot, and sex to me is a way of showing love that you don't want to share with everybody."

Although most of Malcolm's friends aren't virgins, they respect his choice. "Most of my buddies know I'm waiting until I'm married and they're cool with that. They don't give me the lowdown of what they're doing with their partners. At the same time, it's not like I think I'm better than them."

Who Is Leading the Way?

The past few years have seen the creation of many groups that support and celebrate hanging on to one's virginity. One such group, called Clean Teens, advocates sexual abstinence until marriage. Based in Modesto, California, Clean Teens is headed by eighteen-year-old Kirk McCall, who believes that staying a virgin until tying the knot is important due to the potential repercussions of premarital sex: AIDS, other STDs, and unwanted pregnancy.

"I Wasn't Planning on It . . ."

This classic quote comes out of the mouths of 85 percent of the one million teenage girls who get pregnant each year in the United States. Of the total number of sexually active teenage girls, 20 percent become pregnant.

As it turns out, Kirk McCall is not alone in his belief that waiting until marriage is better. Many teen males are shedding their macho image and declaring that virginity is the way to go. This new stance contradicts the stereotype of the teenage guy who will do nearly anything to score.

With more and more provirginity groups cropping up—all declaring that not scoring can be just as cool as going all the way—an increasing number of teenage virgins are speaking out about their choices. Vinnie, whose story you can read on the next page, is typical of many modern-day male virgins.

Vinnie plays football and soccer, drives a sports car, and sometimes gets pretty good grades. One of the most popular guys at his high school, he can usually be found at his locker surrounded by a group of admiring girls. Not only is Vinnie handsome, he is also extremely polite and friendly.

Vinnie is the kind of guy who calls you up, and if he gets your mother on the phone first, says, "Hello, Mrs. Dallio. How are you today? May I please speak with Sylvie? Thanks very much, Mrs. Dallio." He is the class president, too.

Do you think Vinnie sounds like a big stud? Well, in fact, he's a virgin. Until he falls in love, Vinnie's putting sex on the back burner.

Making the decision to remain a virgin—and sticking with it—can be tough. One thing that helps is to be aware of the difference between fact and fiction when it comes to popularly held beliefs about virginity.

Myths About Virginity

- ◆ If you stay a virgin for too long, you won't be able to have kids. (Just plain wrong.)

- ◆ You can tell if someone's a virgin by the way he or she walks. (Yeah, right!)

+ If you wait until you're married to lose your virginity, sex won't hurt. (It may or may not cause discomfort for a female, no matter when it happens.)

+ If your hymen is intact, you can't get pregnant. (Even if your hymen is intact and no penis has entered your vagina, there is a chance that you can still become pregnant if sperm comes in contact with the labia or the vaginal area.)

+ If you have had a Pap smear at the gynecologist's office, you are no longer a virgin. (Losing your virginity involves sexual penetration. Although a Pap smear does involve penetration of the vagina, it is not considered sexual.)

Chapter Four

To Be or Not to Be

You're probably familiar with this famous quote uttered by William Shakespeare's character, Hamlet, in a moment of adolescent indecision (critics believe the prince of Denmark to be in his late teens). Contemporary kids Hamlet's age can relate to both the quote and the accompanying feelings of uncertainty. "To be or not to be" a virgin is a question that many teens inevitably ask themselves.

To "Do It" or Not to "Do It"—That Is the Question

Despite the recent growth of virgin support groups and the coming out of virgins on television, in magazines, and in high schools across North America, there is still a lot of pressure put on adolescents—by their peers, their

It takes a lot of thought to decide if you are ready for sex.

partners, and themselves—to go all the way. However, many teens are told by their families and religious organizations not to have sex at all. With so much pressure, it can be a good idea to sit back and think about what it is that you want. After all, your virginity belongs to you.

If you are unsure whether you are ready to have sex, try asking yourself—and answering honestly—the following questions:

- ◆ Do you have any moral, cultural or religious beliefs that might make the decision to have sex the wrong decision for you?

- ◆ How do you feel about your relationship with your partner? Do you trust and respect him/her?

- What do you think might happen as a result of having sex? How do you think you will feel about your partner afterward? More important, how do you think you will feel about yourself?

- How much do you know about herpes, AIDS, and other STDs? Have you talked about the possibility of STDs and/or pregnancy with your partner? If so, what precautions are each of you willing to take to prevent such situations?

- What would you and your partner do if sex did result in pregnancy or disease?

- Do you, for any reason, feel pressured to have sex—either by your partner or by your friends?

- Do you feel that you and your partner can comfortably make a decision right now as to whether to have sex?

- Can you talk to your partner about your decisions no matter what they are?

If the answer to even one of these questions leaves you with doubt in your mind, you are probably not yet ready to go all the way. Take your time, educate yourself, and prepare yourself for all of the possible consequences of sex—both physical (STDs, AIDS, pregnancy) and emotional (feelings of guilt, regret, strangeness).

Take your time when making any decision about sexual activity.

Talk with your partner and, if you want to, with a close friend, a parent, or another adult whom you respect and trust and with whom you have an open, comfortable relationship. If you prefer some anonymity, there are hotlines and Web sites especially for teens that can advise you (see the resource listings at the back of this book).

Remember that sex can be a positive and beautiful thing, but it is also a serious act that has serious consequences. Once you have lost your virginity, it really is lost—there is no turning back the clock. Your first time is, in many ways, a milestone. It is a moment you will remember for the rest of your life, so it is one that you want to make special for both you and your partner.

Has anyone ever tried to pressure you with one of the following lines?

"But everybody's doing it."

"You say no, but I know you really want it."

"You're not really gay. You just haven't met the right girl yet."

"You mean you're *still* a virgin?"

"What's the matter? Are you a lesbian or something?"

"But we had sex last time!"

"If you love me, you'll do it."

It is essential to be prepared if you and your partner decide to have sex. This means being responsible, taking the proper precautions against STDs and pregnancy, and treating your partner and yourself with respect, caring, and honesty at all times. It also means not rushing into sex, but planning for it.

On the other hand, if you decide not to have sex—at least for a while—there are plenty of ways to express yourself sexually with your partner without having sexual intercourse. There is kissing, massage, mutual masturbation, rubbing, nibbling, and tickling. These and other sensual ways of giving and receiving pleasure are great—and often just as arousing—alternatives to intercourse. Furthermore, they allow you to get to know and become sexually comfortable with your-selves and each other. This way, when you do decide to go all the way—be it with your present partner or someone in the future—you really will be ready.

Teens Talk About Losing Their Virginity

Some Regret It . . .

"I regret losing it because I did it for the wrong reason. I did it only because most of my friends had. I felt like I'd be a big loser if I didn't do it before graduating from high school."

"I regret the way I lost it. I got really wasted one night and it just happened. The only thing I remember is that I lost it to the best friend of my girlfriend at the time. Of course, my girlfriend broke up with me."

"I regret that I didn't take more control. I let the guy manipulate me and when we were done, he just got up and left. I felt so used. I would never again have sex without really knowing the person well."

"I was thirteen, but it wasn't my choice. I was raped by my brother's best friend who was nineteen. I wish my first time could have been special and not emotionally damaging."

Others Don't . . .

"I had heard the first time really hurt and so I was really afraid of the pain. But both my boyfriend and I found some good information and when I really felt ready, we—especially my boyfriend—took it nice and slow. I have to say that my experience was quite exciting. There was a little pain, but it was worth it."

"I don't regret losing my virginity. I was maybe a little young, but I think I would do it the same way if I could. The thing I do regret is not being open. I lied and said it was great because I thought it would make my girlfriend feel better. I didn't realize until we had broken up that I should have told her what I really wanted sexually. She really loved me and would have been happier making me feel good, but I never told her what I wanted."

"I lost my virginity to my boyfriend and I don't regret a thing because it is beautiful when done under the right circumstances."

Chapter Five

Sex and Love

From a mechanical point of view, the acts of having sex and making love are one and the same. However, emotionally there is a big difference between the two. Having sex in itself is nothing special. Ultimately, it is little more than a physical activity. Making love, however, is very special. It occurs when two people who care a great deal about each other and are attracted to each other decide to express their love in an intimate, physical manner.

There are many beautiful ways of expressing love: telling someone you care deeply for him or her; writing a poem, a song, or a letter; making or buying a memorable gift; planning a special trip or outing. You might find all of the above satisfying ways of expressing your strong feelings for the person you love. Or, at some point, you might want to express those feelings in a physical, sexual manner. As are most things in life, sex

43

Enjoying sex involves preparation, such as talking to your partner about your feelings.

can be both good and bad. Enjoying sex—especially the first time—can take some preparation. There are certain things both guys and girls can do to make "losing it" a memorable and pleasurable experience instead of a painful and confusing one.

What Guys Can Do

For a guy, there are several important things to remember when you're preparing for your first time. One is to make sure you have protection—i.e., a condom—and that you know how to use it correctly. (It's surprising how many people don't!) Buy condoms in advance and don't be embarrassed about trying one on—even alone—to get used to the way it feels and to make sure you have the right size. Most condoms come already lubricated. But you might want to use extra lubricant. If so, always use a water-based one and not an oil-based one (such as Vaseline or moisturizers, which can disintegrate a condom's latex). Lubrication will make the first penetration a lot smoother for you and a lot less painful for your partner.

Sex is a lot more than just taking pleasure from your partner and then falling asleep. It is also about giving pleasure to someone you love. Take time to play with and talk to your partner. Many girls might feel nervous about both their bodies and about losing their virginity. So make her feel secure with herself and with you. Making love is much less about actual penetration and

What to Do with a Condom

BEFORE...

- Check that your condoms are still fresh (look at the expiration date) and not squished, scrunched, or victims of the washing machine's rinse cycle. If in doubt, throw them away and start fresh.

- Make sure the penis is hard.

- Open the package carefully so you don't rip the condom.

- Condoms are like socks. Make sure yours isn't inside-out before rolling it on. If at first you don't succeed, try again—with a new condom.

and AFTER...

- Withdraw from your partner while you are still hard. Hold the condom near your testicles so it doesn't slip off. Remove the condom once you are completely out of your partner.

- Throw out the used condom right away. A single condom should never be used more than once.

Check the date on condoms
to see if they have expired.

much more about all of the tenderness and playfulness that lead up to and follow the act. Ultimately, a great lover is someone who knows how to put his partner's pleasure and feelings ahead of his own.

What Girls Can Do

There are several things a girl can do to make her first time a good experience. Of course, one of the foremost is making sure that she will be protected from catching any STDs or getting pregnant. Make sure both you and your guy have condoms and know how to use them.

A big part of enjoying sex is being confident about your body. Many girls feel self-conscious about being naked. This is normal. It takes time to feel at ease. Try doing other things with your partner—massages, baths, naps. This helps to build a sense of intimacy and trust between you. It will also help you to lose some sexual inhibitions.

Some girls feel shy about discovering their own bodies. But if you want to be a good lover who is able to give and receive pleasure without a lot of pain and confusion, it is a good idea to get to know your private parts on your own. Do this not only by looking at yourself, but by touching yourself. This way, you get to know what is what. When you finally do have sex, you will be able to guide your partner, who will probably be quite nervous about the Great Unknown before him. The result? A first time that is much more satisfying and less stressful for both of you.

Having Bad Sex

Just as good sex can be really, really good, bad sex can be a traumatic experience that can hurt you emotionally and even physically. Equally harmful are the psychological effects, which, if left ignored and untreated, can make future close sexual and emotional relationships extremely difficult, or even impossible.

Sex can be bad if you do it for the wrong reasons or without preparing for it. It can be bad if you have it without being truly sure whether you want to. But sex can be truly, catastrophically bad if you are psychologically or physically pressured or forced into it. If someone forces you to have sex against your will, this is called rape. Rape is a crime and there are no two ways about it. And a rapist doesn't have to be a stranger. It can be—and more often than not it is—someone you know and trust. Date rape and acquaintance rape are two very common occurrences.

> *Louise was excited when Bobby invited her to the party at his frat house. Louise was shy and had trouble meeting guys. And Bobby was so hot. Countless girls were always swooning over him.*
>
> *After the two arrived at the party, Bobby ignored Louise. She didn't know anybody there and she wandered around feeling ill at ease. To have something to do, she kept going to the punch bowl, which was full of a drink called Electric*

Jello. It tasted like fruit punch, but she was sure it was full of hard alcohol.

Louise was about to leave when Bobby asked her to dance. They danced a lot and Bobby told Louise how hot he was for her. She remembered them dancing into a darkened bedroom where Bobby started pulling off his clothes and then hers. When she figured out what was happening, Louise was lying on a bed with Bobby on top of her, panting. "Get off me!" she yelled, feeling sick. But Bobby just slapped her and told her to shut up.

The next morning, Louise felt horrible. Her head was splitting and she felt sore around her vagina. When she realized what had happened, and that they hadn't used any protection, Louise began to cry.

Just as serious as rape—and a lot more complicated in many ways—is incest. Incest occurs when you are forced to have sex with a family member. This happens most often to young people, who are sworn never to tell anyone. Often, deeply divided loyalties, fear, and shame make it extremely difficult for victims of such sexual abuse to talk about it. However, keeping such feelings inside can be torture. It also can make it very difficult to develop sexual relationships later in life.

Even if you do consent to have sex, it is not acceptable that your partner hurt you in any way against your will. There is a big difference between a love bite

If you have been abused in any way, seek help immediately.

and a smack in the head. The difference is called physical abuse and it can turn sex into a horrible experience.

If You Are a Victim of Rape, Incest, or Physical Abuse . . .

1. Tell someone you trust.

2. Get help—medical, if you're physically hurt, as well as psychological (a good therapist is essential).

3. Hold on tight to the fact that it is not your fault. You did not ask for it, you do not deserve it, and you are entitled to respect. If you want to, press charges or file a report with the police.

Safe Is Sexy

Many images from popular culture—whether from movies, music videos, or television—link sex with risk-taking and danger. Although this is a romantic notion, it is also pure fiction. Compared with other Western countries, the United States has a high rate of teenage pregnancy. AIDS is the second largest cause of death among young Americans—both gay and straight. And countless teenage girls lose their virginity while passed out drunk or drugged at a party. All of this goes to show that giving in to a moment of passion has consequences that are very real, that are very unpleasant, and which can truly change the rest of your life—for the worse.

That is why, for the first time and every time thereafter, it is essential that you always have safe sex. Being safe does not mean you can't be spontaneous, passionate, or romantic. Nor does it mean planning everything out in advance. But it does mean being informed and prepared for sex—and safely engaging in it. Ultimately, safe sex is the sexiest kind. It frees you from worries and stress, pain and regrets, and allows you to get on with the immediate business at hand.

Safe Sex Is . . .

- Protecting yourself and your partner against STDs (your best bet is a condom). The way to do this is to make sure you don't get anyone else's blood, semen, vaginal fluids, or breast milk in your body

- Always using at least one form of birth control
- Never mixing sexual activity with alcohol or drugs
- Having sex in a clean, comfortable, controlled (and preferably romantic) environment
- Limiting your sexual activities to those that you can do safely, as well as learning to control your sexual behavior
- Keeping the number of sexual partners to a minimum
- Communicating honestly and openly about what you want and don't want both in advance of and during sex

Conclusion

By the time Jimmy had climbed through Jocelyn's bedroom window at 1 AM, Jocelyn had changed her mind. She had realized that she didn't want to have sex—at least not yet, and not with Jimmy. She didn't like it that having sex with Jimmy had to be a guilty secret to hide from her parents. She didn't like all of the worries and stress that the decision to have sex with Jimmy was causing her.

Always respect your partner's wishes; don't pressure him or her.

But most of all, she realized that—although she really did want to have sex—she didn't want to have it right then.

Jocelyn expected Jimmy to be mad at her. But he wasn't. In fact, he seemed sort of relieved. Both Jimmy and Jocelyn decided that there were many other intimate things they could do together: things that would allow them to get to know each other and enjoy each other, without any pressure. Perhaps doing these other things would lead them to have sex. And perhaps it wouldn't. But they did promise each other that they would always be open and talk about their feelings honestly. And that was already something.

Glossary

abstinence   Refraining from having sex.

chastity   Sexual abstinence.

cherry   Slang expression for the hymen.

chlamydia   An infection caused by a bacteria called *Chlamydia trachomatis.* It is one of the most common STDs and, if left untreated, can lead to sterility.

clitoris   A highly sensitive organ in the female, located above and in front of the vaginal entrance.

condom   A sheath that is placed over the erect penis to protect against pregnancy and sexually transmitted diseases.

estrogen   Hormone that is responsible for sexual maturation and regulation of periods in women.

foreplay   Term used to refer to sexual activities other than intercourse.

Pap smear   A test for cervical cancer that is done by examining cells scraped off the cervix during a pelvic examination.

premarital sex   Sexual activity, especially sexual intercourse, before marriage.

safe sex   Sexual activities that do not involve the exchange of bodily fluids. Practiced to prevent the transmission of diseases such as AIDS.

semen   The fluid expelled by the penis during ejaculation, which contains fluids combined from several glands, as well as sperm.

sperm   The male reproductive cell.

testicles   The small, oval sex glands of the male, located in the scrotum, that produce sperm and the sex hormone testosterone.

testosterone   The hormone secreted by the testes that helps to maintain sperm production and sex drive.

vagina   Tube-shaped muscular organ in the female into which the penis is inserted during intercourse and through which a baby passes during birth.

venereal disease   Disease transmitted through sexual contact.

Where to Go for Help

In the United States

National Women's Health Network
514 10th Street NW, Suite 400
Washington, DC 20005
(202) 347-1140

Planned Parenthood Federation of America
810 Seventh Avenue
New York, NY 10019
(800) 230-7526
Facts of Life Hotline: (212) 965-7015
Web site: http://www.ppfa.org

The Rape, Abuse, and Incest National Network
  (RAINN)

635-B Pennsylvania Avenue SE
Washington, DC 20003
(800) 656-HOPE
Web site: http://www.rainn.org
e-mail: RAINNmail@aol.com

Sexuality Information and Education Council of the
    United States (SIECUS)
130 West 42nd Street, Suite 350
New York, NY 10036
(212) 819-9770
Web site: http://www.siecus.org
e-mail: siecus@siecus.org

Violence Against Women Office
801 7th Street NW
Washington, DC 20531
(202) 616-8894
Web site: http://www.usdoj.gov/vawo

In Canada

Kids Help Foundation
National Office
439 University Avenue, Suite 300
Toronto, ON M5G 1Y8
(416) 586-5437

Kids Help Phone
(800) 668-6868
http://kidshelp.sympatico.ca

Lambton Health Unit
Youth Issues
Web site: http://www.lambtonhealth.on.ca/
    youth/index.html
e-mail: lambhlth@ebtech.net

Ottawa Sexual Assault Centre Hotline
(613) 234-2266

Planned Parenthood Federation of Canada
1 Nicholas Street, Suite 430
Ottawa, ON K1N 7B7
(613) 241-4474
Web site: http://www.ppfc.org
e-mail: admin@ppfc.ca

Sexuality Education Resource Centre
Winnepeg Office
555 Broadway Avenue, 2nd Floor
Winnepeg, MB R3C 0W4
(204) 982-7800
Web site: http://www.serc.mb

Web Sites

Chick Click
http://www.chickclick.com

Girl Power
http://www.girlpower.com

Teen Advice Online
http://www.teenadvice.org

For Further Reading

Ayer, Eleanor. *It's Okay to Say No: Choosing Sexual Abstinence*. New York: Rosen Publishing Group, 1999.

Bartle, Nathalie, and Susan Liberman. *Venus in Blue Jeans: Why Mothers and Daughters Need to Talk About Sex*. New York: Houghten Mifflin Co., 1998.

Basso, Michael J. *The Underground Guide to Teenage Sexuality: An Essential Handbook for Today's Teens and Parents*. Minneapolis, MN: Fairview Press, 1997.

Bouris, Karen. *The First Time: What Parents and Teenage Girls Should Know About Losing Your Virginity*. Berkeley, CA: Conari Press, 1995.

Elliott, Leland. *Sex on Campus: The Naked Truth About the Real Sex Lives of College Students*. New York: Random House, 1997.

Mogalia, Ronald. *All About Sex: A Family Resource on Sex and Sexuality*. New York: Planned Parenthood, 1997.

Pogany, Susan Browning. *Sex Smart: 501 Reasons to Hold Off on Sex: A Sexuality Resource for Teenagers.* Minneapolis, MN: Fairview Press, 1998.

Roberts, Tara. *Am I the Last Virgin? Ten African American Reflections on Sex and Love.* New York: Simon and Schuster, 1997.

Index

About the Authors

Michael A. Sommers is a freelance journalist with a master's degree in history and civilization. Raised in Toronto, Canada, he now lives in Brazil. He used to be a virgin, and his younger sister, Annie Leah Sommers, used to be a virgin, too. Annie has master's degrees in children's literature and fine arts. Born in Toronto, she is now an editor and printmaker in New York City. The Sommers siblings have an eighteen-year-old cat named Jesse who lives in Toronto. Early on in life, Jesse decided to abstain from postneutered sex. He will always be a beloved virgin.

Photo Credits

Cover and pp. 2, 15, 37, 39, 44, 47, 51, 54 by Kristen Artz; p.9 © The Everett Collection; p.12 © Custom Medical; p.17 © Corbis; pp. 21, 23, 30 © Super Stock

Design and Layout

Michael J. Caroleo